Cuba

Everything You Need to Know

4

Introduction to Cuba

Welcome to the vibrant world of Cuba, a land of rich history, captivating culture, and unparalleled charm. Situated in the heart of the Caribbean, Cuba has long been a melting pot of influences, shaped by centuries of colonialism, revolution, and resilience.

As you embark on this journey through the pages of this book, prepare to uncover the many facets of this intriguing island nation. From its pre-colonial roots to its modern-day complexities, Cuba offers a tapestry of experiences that will leave an indelible mark on your soul.

First settled by indigenous peoples such as the Taíno and Ciboney, Cuba's earliest inhabitants left behind a legacy of art, agriculture, and spirituality. With the arrival of Spanish explorers in the 15th century, Cuba became a pivotal player in the age of exploration, serving as a strategic hub for trade and conquest.

Under Spanish colonial rule, Cuba flourished as a center of sugar production, fueled by the labor of enslaved Africans brought to the island. This era of prosperity was marred by exploitation and oppression, setting the stage for centuries of struggle for independence.

In the late 19th century, Cuban patriots rose up against Spanish rule, sparking a series of wars for independence that culminated in the Spanish-American War of 1898. With the defeat of Spain, Cuba gained nominal independence, albeit under the shadow of U.S. influence.

The 20th century saw Cuba's transformation into a battleground for competing ideologies, as revolutionaries like Fidel Castro and Che Guevara waged a guerrilla war against the corrupt dictatorship of Fulgencio Batista. In 1959, Castro's revolution triumphed, ushering in a new era of socialist rule and challenging the dominance of Western powers in the region.

The Cuban Revolution sparked both admiration and controversy on the global stage, drawing admiration for its ideals of social justice and equality, while also facing criticism for its authoritarian tendencies and human rights abuses. Despite decades of economic hardship and isolation, Cuba has remained steadfast in its commitment to sovereignty and self-determination.

Today, Cuba stands at a crossroads, as the island grapples with the complexities of modernization and globalization. From its vibrant cities to its pristine beaches, Cuba offers a treasure trove of experiences for intrepid travelers and curious adventurers alike.

So join me as we delve deep into the heart and soul of Cuba, exploring its history, culture, and people with open minds and open hearts. Welcome to the enchanting world of Cuba – a land of contradictions, complexities, and endless possibilities.

Pre-Colonial Cuba: Origins and Indigenous Cultures

Long before the arrival of European explorers, the island of Cuba was inhabited by indigenous peoples who had established thriving communities across the land. These early inhabitants, known as the Taíno and Ciboney, were part of the larger Arawak-speaking population that had spread throughout the Caribbean.

The origins of these indigenous cultures can be traced back thousands of years, to the migration of peoples from South America to the islands of the Caribbean. The Taíno, in particular, are believed to have migrated to Cuba from regions such as present-day Venezuela and Colombia, bringing with them a rich cultural heritage that would shape the island's history for centuries to come.

Life for the indigenous peoples of pre-colonial Cuba revolved around agriculture, fishing, and hunting, as they established settlements along the coastlines and rivers of the island. They cultivated crops such as maize, cassava, and sweet potatoes, using advanced agricultural techniques to maximize their yields.

The Taíno and Ciboney lived in villages governed by chieftains, who held authority over their respective communities. Social structure was hierarchical, with individuals occupying different roles based on factors such as age, gender, and lineage. Religion played a central role in Taíno society, with spiritual beliefs centered around the worship of nature spirits and ancestors.

Art and craftsmanship flourished among the indigenous peoples of Cuba, as evidenced by the intricate pottery, weaving, and carvings produced by Taíno artisans. Their artistic expressions reflected a deep connection to the natural world, with motifs inspired by animals, plants, and celestial bodies.

Trade networks crisscrossed the Caribbean, connecting the indigenous peoples of Cuba with neighboring islands such as Hispaniola and Jamaica. These networks facilitated the exchange of goods, ideas, and cultural practices, contributing to the diversity and richness of Caribbean civilization.

Despite their achievements, the indigenous peoples of pre-colonial Cuba faced numerous challenges, including conflict with rival groups, natural disasters, and diseases introduced by European contact. The arrival of Spanish explorers in the late 15th century would ultimately irrevocably alter the course of history for the indigenous peoples of Cuba, as they were subjected to colonization, exploitation, and ultimately, extinction. Yet, their legacy lives on in the cultural heritage of modern-day Cuba, serving as a testament to the resilience and ingenuity of the island's original inhabitants.

Spanish Colonial Rule: Conquest and Colonization

The era of Spanish colonial rule in Cuba began with the arrival of Christopher Columbus on the island's shores during his first voyage to the New World in 1492. Initially, Columbus claimed Cuba for the Spanish crown, but it wasn't until 1511 that Spanish colonization efforts truly took hold under the leadership of Diego Velázquez de Cuéllar.

Velázquez established the first permanent Spanish settlement in Cuba, founding the town of Baracoa on the island's northeastern coast. This marked the beginning of a process of conquest and colonization that would profoundly shape the course of Cuban history for centuries to come.

Spanish colonization of Cuba was driven by a desire for wealth and power, with Spanish conquistadors seeking to exploit the island's abundant natural resources, including gold, silver, and fertile land suitable for agriculture. They also sought to convert the indigenous population to Christianity, viewing them as potential subjects of the Spanish crown.

The Spanish colonial administration in Cuba was characterized by a system of encomienda, which granted Spanish settlers the right to extract tribute and labor from the indigenous peoples in exchange for protection and Christian instruction. This system often led to the exploitation and abuse of the indigenous population, as they were forced to work on Spanish-owned plantations and in mines under harsh conditions.

The introduction of African slavery further fueled the growth of the Cuban economy, as enslaved Africans were brought to the island to work on sugar plantations and in other industries. By the 18th century, Cuba had become one of the largest producers of sugar in the world, with enslaved Africans comprising the majority of the island's population.

Spanish colonial rule in Cuba was also marked by periods of conflict and resistance, as indigenous peoples and enslaved Africans fought against their oppressors in a series of rebellions and uprisings. One of the most notable of these rebellions was the Ten Years' War (1868-1878), which sought to end Spanish colonial rule and achieve independence for Cuba.

Despite these challenges, Spanish colonial rule in Cuba endured for centuries, shaping the island's society, economy, and culture in profound ways. The legacy of Spanish colonization can still be seen in the architecture, language, and traditions of modern-day Cuba, serving as a reminder of the island's complex and tumultuous history.

Cuba's Struggle for Independence: Wars and Revolutions

Cuba's struggle for independence was a tumultuous and multifaceted journey, marked by wars, revolutions, and the unyielding determination of its people to break free from colonial oppression. The seeds of resistance were sown in the early 19th century, as Cuban patriots began to agitate for greater autonomy and self-determination in the face of Spanish colonial rule.

One of the earliest expressions of this resistance was the Conspiracy of La Escalera in 1844, a failed plot to overthrow Spanish authorities and establish an independent republic in Cuba. Despite its failure, the Conspiracy of La Escalera served as a harbinger of the unrest and discontent that would simmer beneath the surface of Cuban society for decades to come.

The quest for independence gained momentum in the mid-19th century, fueled by a wave of nationalist fervor and inspired by the success of independence movements in other Latin American countries. In 1868, Cuban patriot Carlos Manuel de Céspedes proclaimed the Grito de Yara, igniting the flames of revolution and launching the Ten Years' War against Spanish colonial rule.

14

The Ten Years' War was a protracted and bloody conflict that exacted a heavy toll on both sides, as Cuban insurgents fought valiantly against the well-equipped forces of the Spanish crown. Despite their efforts, however, the Ten Years' War ultimately ended in defeat for the Cuban rebels, as they were unable to overcome the superior firepower and resources of the Spanish army.

The failure of the Ten Years' War did not extinguish the flame of Cuban nationalism, however, and in 1895, another revolutionary leader emerged to reignite the struggle for independence. José Martí, a poet, and philosopher, sought to unite Cubans of all backgrounds in a common cause against Spanish colonialism, declaring that "Cuba must be free, at whatever cost."

Martí's vision inspired a new generation of revolutionaries, including the charismatic guerrilla leader, Antonio Maceo, who led a series of daring raids and guerrilla campaigns against Spanish forces in the eastern provinces of Cuba. The resulting conflict, known as the Cuban War of Independence or the Spanish-American War, would ultimately culminate in the defeat of Spanish forces and the establishment of an independent republic in Cuba.

The Spanish-American War was a turning point in Cuban history, as it not only brought an end to Spanish colonial rule but also thrust Cuba into the sphere of American influence. In 1902, Cuba formally gained independence from Spain, only to become a de facto protectorate of the United States under the terms of the Platt Amendment.

Despite the challenges and setbacks that accompanied its struggle for independence, Cuba emerged from the crucible of war with a newfound sense of national identity and purpose. The legacy of its revolutionary heroes, from Céspedes and Martí to Maceo and Castro, continues to inspire future generations of Cubans as they navigate the complexities of their nation's history and identity.

The Rise of Fidel Castro: Revolution and Socialist Ideals

The rise of Fidel Castro marked a pivotal moment in Cuban history, as the charismatic revolutionary leader emerged from the shadows to challenge the entrenched power structures of the island's ruling elite. Born into a middle-class family in rural Cuba in 1926, Castro was educated in Havana and later studied law at the University of Havana, where he became involved in student politics and leftist activism.

Castro's political awakening was shaped by the turbulent events of his time, including the overthrow of President Gerardo Machado in 1933 and the rise of authoritarian regimes in Latin America. Inspired by the ideals of social justice and equality, Castro became increasingly disillusioned with the corruption and inequality that plagued Cuban society, laying the groundwork for his revolutionary aspirations.

In 1953, Castro launched a bold and audacious attack on the Moncada Barracks in Santiago de Cuba, in an ill-fated attempt to overthrow the regime of dictator Fulgencio Batista. Although the attack failed and Castro was arrested and imprisoned, his defiant courtroom speech, known as "History Will Absolve Me," captured the imagination of the Cuban people and catapulted him to national prominence as a symbol of resistance against Batista's tyranny.

After serving two years in prison, Castro was released as part of a general amnesty and went into exile in Mexico, where he began to organize a revolutionary movement aimed at overthrowing the Batista regime. In 1956, Castro and a small band of followers, including the Argentine revolutionary Che Guevara, landed in Cuba aboard the yacht Granma, sparking the beginning of the Cuban Revolution.

For the next two years, Castro and his guerrilla fighters waged a guerrilla war against Batista's forces in the mountains of eastern Cuba, gaining support from peasants, workers, and intellectuals disillusioned with the Batista regime. Despite facing overwhelming odds and constant harassment from government forces, Castro's guerrillas persevered, slowly gaining ground and momentum as they marched towards victory.

On January 1, 1959, Batista fled Cuba in the face of advancing rebel forces, and Castro's guerrillas entered Havana in triumph, bringing an end to Batista's dictatorship and marking the beginning of a new era in Cuban history. Castro wasted no time in consolidating his power, instituting sweeping reforms aimed at transforming Cuban society along socialist lines.

Under Castro's leadership, Cuba embarked on a radical program of social and economic transformation, nationalizing key industries, redistributing land to peasants, and implementing universal healthcare and education programs. Castro's government also forged close ties with the Soviet Union, adopting Marxist-Leninist ideology and aligning Cuba firmly within the socialist bloc.

Castro's revolutionary zeal and commitment to socialist ideals earned him both admirers and detractors at home and abroad. While supporters praised him as a visionary leader who had liberated Cuba from the shackles of imperialism and exploitation, critics accused him of authoritarianism, human rights abuses, and economic mismanagement.

Despite facing numerous challenges and setbacks, including the failed Bay of Pigs invasion in 1961 and the Cuban Missile Crisis in 1962, Castro remained firmly in power for over five decades, until his retirement due to health reasons in 2008. His legacy continues to loom large in Cuban politics and society, as the island grapples with the complexities of its revolutionary past and uncertain future.

Post-Revolution Cuba: The Castro Era and Beyond

In the aftermath of the Cuban Revolution, the island entered a new chapter in its history, defined by the leadership of Fidel Castro and his vision of a socialist society. Castro wasted no time in implementing sweeping reforms aimed at reshaping Cuban society along socialist lines, including the nationalization of key industries, the redistribution of land, and the establishment of universal healthcare and education programs.

During the early years of the Castro era, Cuba enjoyed a period of economic growth and social progress, as the government invested heavily in infrastructure, healthcare, and education. Literacy rates soared, healthcare outcomes improved, and access to basic services expanded to even the most remote corners of the island.

However, Castro's revolutionary zeal and commitment to socialist ideology also drew the ire of the United States, which viewed Cuba as a threat to its interests in the Western Hemisphere. In response to Castro's nationalization of American-owned businesses and alignment with the Soviet Union, the United States imposed a trade embargo on Cuba in 1960, severing diplomatic ties and launching a campaign of economic and political isolation that would last for decades.

The embargo, combined with the collapse of the Soviet Union in the early 1990s, dealt a severe blow to the Cuban economy, plunging the island into a period of economic hardship known as the "Special Period." During this time, Cuba faced shortages of food, fuel, and other essential goods, leading to widespread deprivation and suffering among the population.

Despite these challenges, Castro's government managed to weather the storm, implementing a series of economic reforms aimed at opening up the Cuban economy to foreign investment and tourism. These reforms, coupled with the resilience and ingenuity of the Cuban people, helped to alleviate some of the worst effects of the Special Period and lay the groundwork for Cuba's economic recovery in the years that followed.

Throughout the Castro era, Cuba remained a key player on the world stage, championing anti-imperialist and socialist causes in Latin America and beyond. Castro's government provided support to revolutionary movements in countries such as Nicaragua, Angola, and Venezuela, earning him both admirers and critics on the global stage.

In 2006, Fidel Castro's health began to deteriorate, leading him to transfer power to his younger brother, Raúl Castro, who served as interim president until formally assuming the presidency in 2008. Under Raúl's leadership, Cuba embarked on a new phase of economic reform, aimed at modernizing the island's socialist economy and attracting foreign investment.

In 2014, Raúl Castro announced a historic thaw in relations with the United States, leading to the restoration of diplomatic ties and the easing of some travel and trade restrictions. The move was hailed as a significant step towards normalization between the two longtime adversaries, although tensions between the two countries persist to this day.

As Cuba looks towards the future, it faces a host of challenges and opportunities, from economic reform and political transition to the preservation of its revolutionary legacy and national identity. Whether the island will continue on its socialist path or embrace new models of governance remains uncertain, but one thing is clear: the legacy of the Castro era will continue to shape the destiny of Cuba for generations to come.

Cuba-U.S. Relations: From Friendship to Friction

The relationship between Cuba and the United States has been a complex and often contentious one, shaped by a combination of historical, political, and ideological factors. In the early years of its independence, Cuba enjoyed close ties with the United States, which viewed the island as a strategic ally in the Caribbean and a lucrative market for American goods.

However, tensions began to emerge in the late 19th and early 20th centuries, as the United States sought to assert its dominance in the region through policies such as the Platt Amendment, which granted the U.S. the right to intervene in Cuban affairs to protect American interests. Despite achieving nominal independence in 1902, Cuba remained effectively under the influence of the United States, with American companies controlling key industries such as sugar and tobacco.

The relationship between Cuba and the United States took a dramatic turn in 1959, with the triumph of the Cuban Revolution and the rise to power of Fidel Castro. Castro's revolutionary government quickly moved to nationalize American-owned businesses and implement sweeping reforms aimed at redistributing wealth

23

and power in Cuban society. These actions drew the ire of the United States, which viewed Castro's government as a threat to its interests in the region.

In response to Castro's nationalization of American assets, the United States imposed a trade embargo on Cuba in 1960, severing diplomatic ties and launching a campaign of economic and political isolation that would last for decades. The embargo, combined with the failed Bay of Pigs invasion in 1961 and the Cuban Missile Crisis in 1962, further exacerbated tensions between the two countries and pushed them to the brink of war.

Despite periodic attempts at rapprochement, including the establishment of diplomatic interests sections in Havana and Washington in the 1970s and the signing of migration agreements in the 1990s, Cuba-U.S. relations remained strained throughout much of the 20th century. The collapse of the Soviet Union in the early 1990s dealt a severe blow to the Cuban economy, leading to a period of economic hardship known as the "Special Period."

In 2014, the relationship between Cuba and the United States underwent a historic thaw, with the announcement of plans to restore diplomatic ties and ease travel and trade restrictions. The move was hailed as a significant step towards normalization between the two longtime adversaries, although tensions between the two countries persist to this day, particularly over issues such as human rights, democracy, and the continued existence of the embargo.

As Cuba looks towards the future, the relationship between the island nation and its northern neighbor remains uncertain, with both countries grappling with the legacy of their turbulent past and seeking to chart a new course based on mutual respect and cooperation. Whether they can overcome their differences and build a relationship based on trust and partnership remains to be seen, but one thing is clear: the history of Cuba-U.S. relations is a testament to the complexities of international diplomacy and the enduring power of ideology and geopolitics.

Cuban Economy: Challenges and Transformations

The Cuban economy has undergone significant challenges and transformations throughout its history, shaped by factors such as colonialism, revolution, and international geopolitics. Prior to the Cuban Revolution of 1959, the island's economy was largely agrarian, with sugar production serving as the backbone of the economy. Under Spanish colonial rule, Cuba became one of the world's leading producers of sugar, relying heavily on enslaved African labor to fuel its lucrative sugar industry.

Following the triumph of the Cuban Revolution, Fidel Castro's government implemented a series of radical reforms aimed at transforming the economy along socialist lines. Key industries, including sugar, banking, and utilities, were nationalized, and land was redistributed to peasants in an effort to achieve greater social and economic equality.

However, the nationalization of American-owned businesses and the imposition of trade restrictions by the United States dealt a severe blow to the Cuban economy, leading to a period of economic hardship known as the "Special Period" in the 1990s. The collapse of the Soviet Union, Cuba's main trading partner and source of economic support, further exacerbated the island's economic woes, plunging it into a deep economic crisis.

In response to the challenges posed by the Special Period, the Cuban government implemented a series of economic reforms aimed at opening up the economy to foreign investment and market forces. These reforms, known as the "updating" of the Cuban economic model, included measures such as the legalization of small private businesses, the expansion of tourism, and the encouragement of foreign investment in key sectors such as tourism, biotechnology, and renewable energy.

Despite these reforms, the Cuban economy continues to face numerous challenges, including inefficiency, corruption, and a bloated state bureaucracy. The dual currency system, which includes both the Cuban peso (CUP) and the convertible peso (CUC), has also created distortions and inefficiencies in the economy, hindering economic growth and development.

In recent years, the Cuban government has sought to attract foreign investment and modernize key sectors of the economy, including agriculture, manufacturing, and telecommunications. However, progress has been slow, hampered by bureaucratic red tape, a lack of infrastructure, and the continued presence of U.S. trade restrictions.

As Cuba looks towards the future, the challenges and opportunities facing its economy are manifold. Despite its rich natural resources, educated workforce, and strategic location in the Caribbean, the Cuban economy remains mired in inefficiency and stagnation. However, with the right combination of policies and reforms, Cuba has the potential to unlock its economic potential and achieve sustainable growth and development in the years to come.

Cuban Society: Diversity and Social Dynamics

Cuban society is a vibrant tapestry woven from a diverse array of cultural influences, shaped by centuries of migration, colonization, and revolution. At its core, Cuban society is characterized by a rich blend of African, European, and indigenous heritage, reflected in its music, art, cuisine, and customs.

One of the defining features of Cuban society is its racial and ethnic diversity. The island's population is comprised of people of African, European, and indigenous descent, with each group contributing to the unique cultural mosaic that defines Cuban identity. Despite the legacy of slavery and colonialism, Cuba has made strides towards racial equality, with policies aimed at promoting racial integration and combating discrimination.

Cuban society is also marked by its strong sense of community and solidarity. Familial ties are deeply ingrained in Cuban culture, with extended families often living together and providing support to one another in times of need. Community organizations known as "Committees for the Defense of the Revolution" (CDRs) play a central role in Cuban society, fostering a sense of collective responsibility and social cohesion.

Religion is another important aspect of Cuban society, with Catholicism being the dominant faith, influenced by African and indigenous spiritual beliefs. Santería, a syncretic religion that blends Catholicism with West African Yoruba traditions, is widely practiced in Cuba and plays a significant role in shaping cultural practices and rituals.

Cuban society is also known for its passion for music, dance, and sports. Music permeates every aspect of Cuban life, from the lively rhythms of salsa and son to the soulful melodies of bolero and trova. Dance is an integral part of Cuban culture, with styles such as salsa, rumba, and mambo captivating audiences around the world. Sports, particularly baseball, are a source of national pride and identity, with Cuba producing some of the world's greatest athletes.

Despite its many strengths, Cuban society also faces numerous challenges, including economic hardship, political repression, and limited access to resources and opportunities. The government's tight control over the media and civil society has led to restrictions on freedom of expression and assembly, stifling dissent and political activism.

In recent years, however, there have been signs of change and evolution in Cuban society, driven in part by economic reforms and increased engagement with the outside world. The rise of entrepreneurship and the growth of the private sector have led to greater economic dynamism and social mobility, albeit with uneven results.

As Cuba continues to navigate the complexities of its social dynamics, the resilience and ingenuity of its people remain its greatest asset. Despite the challenges they face, Cubans are renowned for their warmth, hospitality, and zest for life, qualities that have helped them persevere in the face of adversity and uncertainty.

Cuban Cuisine: Flavors of the Tropics

Cuban cuisine is a delicious reflection of the island's rich cultural heritage, blending indigenous, African, Spanish, and Caribbean influences into a tantalizing array of flavors and textures. At the heart of Cuban cuisine is a focus on fresh, locally sourced ingredients, including tropical fruits, root vegetables, seafood, and meats.

One of the most iconic dishes in Cuban cuisine is ropa vieja, a savory stew made from shredded beef simmered in a rich tomato sauce with onions, peppers, and spices. Another popular dish is arroz con pollo, a hearty combination of rice, chicken, and vegetables cooked in a flavorful broth. Both dishes showcase the bold flavors and vibrant colors that define Cuban cooking.

Seafood also plays a prominent role in Cuban cuisine, thanks to the island's abundant coastal waters. Dishes such as ceviche, made from marinated raw fish or seafood, and camarones al ajillo, shrimp cooked in a garlic-infused sauce, highlight the freshness and simplicity of Cuban seafood preparations.

Plantains, a starchy tropical fruit similar to bananas, are a staple ingredient in Cuban cuisine and can be prepared in a variety of ways. Tostones, or twice-fried plantains, are a popular side dish, while maduros, sweet ripe plantains caramelized in sugar, are often served as a dessert or snack.

Cuban cuisine is also known for its use of spices and seasonings, including cumin, oregano, garlic, and citrus. These bold flavors infuse dishes such as picadillo, a savory ground beef hash seasoned with onions, peppers, and olives, and mojo, a tangy marinade made from citrus juice, garlic, and herbs.

No discussion of Cuban cuisine would be complete without mentioning its iconic beverages. Cuba is famous for its rum, which is used to make refreshing cocktails such as the mojito, daiquiri, and Cuba libre. Coffee is another beloved beverage in Cuban culture, with strong, dark espresso served piping hot and often sweetened with sugar.

In recent years, Cuban cuisine has gained international recognition and acclaim, thanks in part to the efforts of chefs and restaurateurs both on the island and abroad. Cuban restaurants can now be found in cities around the world, serving up traditional dishes with a modern twist and introducing new audiences to the vibrant flavors of the tropics. Whether enjoyed at home or in a restaurant, Cuban cuisine offers a tantalizing taste of the island's rich culinary heritage.

Wildlife of Cuba: Biodiversity in the Caribbean

The wildlife of Cuba is as diverse and captivating as the island's rich cultural heritage. Situated in the heart of the Caribbean, Cuba boasts a wealth of ecosystems, from lush tropical rainforests to pristine coral reefs, providing a habitat for a wide variety of plant and animal species. One of the most iconic inhabitants of Cuban forests is the Cuban trogon, a colorful bird known for its vibrant plumage and distinctive call.

The island is also home to a variety of endemic species, found nowhere else in the world, including the Cuban solenodon, a rare insectivore with a unique venomous bite. In addition to its terrestrial biodiversity, Cuba is surrounded by rich marine environments, teeming with life. Coral reefs off the coast of Cuba are home to a dazzling array of marine species, including colorful fish, sea turtles, and sharks. The Jardines de la Reina, or Gardens of the Queen, is a protected marine reserve off the southern coast of Cuba, renowned for its pristine coral reefs and abundant marine life. In the wetlands and mangrove forests of Cuba, visitors can encounter a variety of bird species, including flamingos, herons, and ibises.

The Zapata Swamp, located on the southern coast of Cuba, is the largest wetland in the Caribbean and serves as an important habitat for migratory birds and endemic species. Despite its wealth of biodiversity, Cuba faces numerous challenges to conservation, including habitat destruction, pollution, and climate change. Efforts to protect and preserve Cuba's natural heritage are ongoing, with the Cuban government and conservation organizations working to establish protected areas, promote sustainable tourism, and raise awareness about the importance of biodiversity conservation.

As Cuba continues to navigate the complexities of development and environmental stewardship, the preservation of its wildlife and natural landscapes remains a critical priority for the island and the world.

Havana: Jewel of the Caribbean

Havana, the capital city of Cuba, stands as a vibrant and eclectic blend of history, culture, and architecture, earning its reputation as the "Jewel of the Caribbean." Founded in 1519 by Spanish conquistadors, Havana quickly grew into one of the wealthiest and most important cities in the New World, serving as a key hub for trade and commerce between Europe, the Americas, and beyond. The city's strategic location on the northern coast of Cuba made it a natural gateway to the Caribbean, attracting merchants, adventurers, and explorers from around the globe.

Throughout its long and storied history, Havana has been shaped by a diverse array of cultural influences, including Spanish, African, and indigenous traditions. This rich cultural tapestry is reflected in the city's architecture, with colorful colonial-era buildings lining its cobblestone streets and grand plazas. The historic center of Havana, known as Old Havana (Habana Vieja), is a UNESCO World Heritage Site, renowned for its well-preserved colonial architecture and charming ambiance.

One of the most iconic landmarks in Havana is the Malecón, a seaside promenade that stretches for several kilometers along the city's waterfront.

Lined with historic buildings, restaurants, and cafes, the Malecón is a popular gathering spot for locals and visitors alike, offering stunning views of the Caribbean Sea and the city skyline.

Havana is also home to a wealth of cultural attractions, including museums, theaters, and art galleries. The Museo Nacional de Bellas Artes (National Museum of Fine Arts) houses an impressive collection of Cuban art, spanning centuries of artistic expression. The Gran Teatro de La Habana (Great Theatre of Havana), with its neoclassical facade and ornate interiors, is a testament to the city's rich cultural heritage and serves as a venue for opera, ballet, and other performing arts.

In addition to its cultural attractions, Havana is known for its vibrant nightlife, with lively bars, clubs, and music venues scattered throughout the city. From traditional Cuban music such as son and salsa to contemporary genres like reggaeton and hip-hop, Havana pulsates with rhythm and energy, inviting visitors to dance the night away in its streets and squares.

Despite its charm and beauty, Havana also bears the scars of its tumultuous past, from the decay and neglect that have plagued many of its historic buildings to the challenges of economic hardship and political repression. However, in recent years, Havana has experienced a renaissance, with renewed investment in infrastructure, tourism, and cultural preservation breathing new life into the city and revitalizing its neighborhoods.

As Havana continues to evolve and transform in the 21st century, it remains a captivating destination for travelers seeking to explore the rich history, vibrant culture, and timeless beauty of the Caribbean's most enchanting city.

Santiago de Cuba: Cradle of the Revolution

Santiago de Cuba, nestled on the southeastern coast of the island, holds a special place in the history of Cuba as the Cradle of the Revolution. Steeped in tradition and infused with revolutionary spirit, Santiago de Cuba has played a pivotal role in shaping the destiny of the nation. Founded in 1515 by Spanish conquistadors, Santiago de Cuba is one of the oldest cities in the Americas, boasting a rich cultural heritage that spans centuries. The city's strategic location made it a key center of trade and commerce in the colonial era, serving as a gateway to the Caribbean and the rest of the New World.

Throughout its history, Santiago de Cuba has been a hotbed of political activism and social change, with a long tradition of resistance against colonial rule and oppression. It was in Santiago de Cuba that the seeds of the Cuban Revolution were first sown, with revolutionary leaders such as Fidel Castro, Raúl Castro, and Ernesto "Che" Guevara launching their revolutionary campaigns from the city's rugged mountains and dense forests.

One of the most significant events in Santiago de Cuba's revolutionary history was the attack on the Moncada Barracks on July 26, 1953. Led by Fidel Castro and a band of revolutionaries, the attack marked the beginning of the armed struggle against the dictatorship of Fulgencio Batista and served as a catalyst for the Cuban Revolution. Although the attack ultimately failed, it galvanized support for the revolutionary cause and laid the groundwork for the eventual overthrow of the Batista regime.

Santiago de Cuba was also the site of the final battle of the Cuban Revolution, with revolutionary forces led by Fidel Castro and Che Guevara defeating Batista's army in a decisive victory that culminated in the triumphal entry of rebel forces into Havana on January 1, 1959. The victory in Santiago de Cuba marked the end of Batista's dictatorship and the beginning of a new era in Cuban history.

Today, Santiago de Cuba remains a vibrant and dynamic city, pulsating with the rhythms of Afro-Cuban music, dance, and culture. The city's lively streets and colorful neighborhoods are a testament to its resilience and spirit, reflecting a proud heritage of struggle and triumph. From its historic plazas and colonial-era buildings to its bustling markets and lively carnivals, Santiago de Cuba continues to inspire and captivate visitors from around the world, offering a glimpse into the heart and soul of the Cuban Revolution.

Trinidad: Colonial Charm and UNESCO Heritage

Nestled on the southern coast of Cuba, Trinidad is a captivating blend of colonial charm and UNESCO World Heritage status. Founded in 1514 by Spanish conquistadors, Trinidad quickly grew into one of the wealthiest and most important cities in colonial Cuba, thanks to its strategic location and thriving sugar industry. The city's historic center, with its cobblestone streets, pastel-colored buildings, and well-preserved colonial architecture, offers a glimpse into Cuba's colonial past, earning it UNESCO World Heritage status in 1988.

Trinidad's colonial-era mansions, known as "palacios," are among the city's most iconic landmarks, with ornate facades, wrought-iron balconies, and lush interior courtyards that speak to the wealth and sophistication of the city's former elite. The Plaza Mayor, the main square in Trinidad, is a focal point of the city's historic center, surrounded by grand colonial buildings and bustling with activity.

In addition to its architectural treasures, Trinidad is also known for its vibrant cultural scene, with museums, art galleries, and music venues scattered throughout the city. The Museo Romántico, housed in a beautifully restored colonial mansion, offers a glimpse into the opulent lifestyle of Trinidad's 19th-century elite, while the Museo

Nacional de la Lucha Contra Bandidos explores the city's revolutionary history.

Trinidad's cultural heritage is also reflected in its music and dance traditions, with lively performances of traditional Cuban music such as son, salsa, and rumba filling the city's streets and squares. The Casa de la Música, located in the heart of Trinidad, is a popular venue for live music and dancing, drawing locals and visitors alike with its infectious rhythms and lively atmosphere.

Beyond its cultural attractions, Trinidad is also blessed with natural beauty, with pristine beaches, lush mountains, and picturesque valleys just a short drive from the city center. The nearby Valle de los Ingenios, or Valley of the Sugar Mills, is a UNESCO World Heritage site in its own right, home to a collection of historic sugar plantations and scenic landscapes that offer a glimpse into Cuba's colonial-era sugar industry.

Today, Trinidad continues to enchant and inspire visitors with its timeless charm, offering a glimpse into Cuba's rich history and cultural heritage. Whether strolling through its historic streets, soaking up the sun on its pristine beaches, or dancing the night away to the rhythm of Cuban music, Trinidad offers a truly unforgettable experience for travelers seeking to explore the beauty and diversity of the Caribbean.

Cienfuegos: Pearl of the South

Situated on the southern coast of Cuba, Cienfuegos shines as the "Pearl of the South," boasting a unique blend of French colonial architecture, rich cultural heritage, and natural beauty. Founded in 1819 by French settlers, Cienfuegos bears the unmistakable imprint of its European roots, with elegant boulevards, neoclassical buildings, and leafy plazas that evoke the charm of Old World Europe.

The city's historic center, known as the "Centro Histórico," is a UNESCO World Heritage Site, recognized for its well-preserved colonial architecture and urban design. The Parque José Martí, the main square in Cienfuegos, is a focal point of the city's historic center, surrounded by grand buildings such as the Palacio de Gobierno and the Teatro Tomás Terry, both prime examples of neoclassical architecture.

Cienfuegos is also known for its vibrant cultural scene, with museums, art galleries, and theaters showcasing the city's rich artistic heritage. The Museo Provincial, housed in a beautifully restored colonial mansion, offers a fascinating glimpse into the history and culture of Cienfuegos, while the Benny Moré Art Center celebrates the life and legacy of the city's most famous son, the legendary Cuban musician Benny Moré.

In addition to its cultural attractions, Cienfuegos is blessed with natural beauty, with pristine beaches, crystal-clear waters, and lush mountains just a short drive from the city center. The nearby Jardín Botánico de Cienfuegos, or Cienfuegos Botanical Garden, is one of the largest and most diverse botanical gardens in Cuba, home to a vast collection of tropical plants and flowers from around the world.

Cienfuegos is also a gateway to the spectacular landscapes of the Cienaga de Zapata, or Zapata Swamp, one of the largest wetlands in the Caribbean and a UNESCO Biosphere Reserve. The swamp is home to a diverse array of wildlife, including crocodiles, flamingos, and the endangered Cuban crocodile, as well as pristine beaches and coral reefs that offer excellent opportunities for snorkeling and scuba diving.

Today, Cienfuegos continues to enchant and inspire visitors with its timeless beauty, offering a glimpse into Cuba's rich history, culture, and natural heritage. Whether exploring its historic streets, lounging on its sun-kissed beaches, or immersing oneself in its vibrant cultural scene, Cienfuegos offers a truly unforgettable experience for travelers seeking to discover the beauty and diversity of the Caribbean.

Varadero: Sun, Sand, and Serenity

Varadero, known as the "Pearl of the North," is Cuba's premier beach resort destination, renowned for its pristine white sands, turquoise waters, and laid-back atmosphere. Situated on the Hicacos Peninsula, Varadero stretches for over 20 kilometers along Cuba's northern coast, offering visitors a paradise of sun, sand, and serenity.

The origins of Varadero as a tourist destination date back to the early 20th century when American millionaires began to flock to the area in search of luxury and relaxation. Since then, Varadero has grown into one of the most popular tourist destinations in the Caribbean, attracting visitors from around the world with its stunning beaches, world-class resorts, and vibrant nightlife.

Varadero's main attraction is its breathtaking beaches, which rank among the finest in the Caribbean. With powdery white sands and crystal-clear waters, Varadero's beaches offer the perfect setting for swimming, sunbathing, and water sports such as snorkeling, diving, and sailing. The calm, shallow waters of Varadero Bay are ideal for families with children, while more adventurous travelers can explore the nearby coral reefs and underwater caves.

In addition to its beaches, Varadero is home to a wealth of cultural and recreational attractions. The

Varadero Golf Club, designed by renowned architect Les Furber, offers an 18-hole championship golf course with stunning views of the Caribbean Sea. The Varahicacos Ecological Reserve, located at the eastern end of the peninsula, is a protected area of mangrove forests, caves, and coastal scrubland, home to a variety of bird and plant species.

Varadero's nightlife is also a major draw for visitors, with a wide range of bars, clubs, and restaurants catering to every taste and budget. From lively beachfront discos to intimate jazz clubs, Varadero offers something for everyone, ensuring that the party never stops in this tropical paradise.

For those seeking a break from the sun and sand, Varadero offers plenty of opportunities for exploration and adventure. Day trips to nearby attractions such as the colonial city of Matanzas, the historic Bay of Pigs, and the vibrant city of Havana are easily accessible from Varadero, allowing visitors to experience the rich culture and history of Cuba beyond the beach.

Whether lounging on the beach, exploring the natural beauty of the surrounding area, or dancing the night away under the stars, Varadero offers the ultimate escape for travelers seeking relaxation, adventure, and unforgettable memories in the Caribbean.

Viñales: Nature and Agriculture in Harmony

Nestled in the picturesque Viñales Valley, Viñales is a tranquil oasis where nature and agriculture coexist in perfect harmony. Located in the western province of Pinar del Río, Viñales is renowned for its stunning natural landscapes, fertile tobacco fields, and traditional farming practices that have remained unchanged for centuries.

The Viñales Valley, designated a UNESCO World Heritage Site in 1999, is characterized by its unique karst formations known as mogotes, which rise dramatically from the valley floor, creating a breathtaking backdrop of limestone cliffs and lush greenery. The valley's fertile soil and favorable climate make it an ideal location for agriculture, particularly tobacco cultivation, which has been practiced in the region for generations.

Tobacco farming is at the heart of Viñales' agricultural heritage, with small family-owned farms known as "vegas" dotting the landscape. Visitors to Viñales can explore these traditional tobacco farms, where skilled farmers cultivate and harvest tobacco using age-old techniques passed down through generations. Guided tours offer visitors the opportunity to learn about the

47

entire process of tobacco production, from planting and harvesting to curing and rolling.

In addition to tobacco, Viñales is also known for its production of other crops such as coffee, fruits, and vegetables, which thrive in the valley's fertile soil and mild climate. Organic farming practices are common in Viñales, with many farmers eschewing synthetic fertilizers and pesticides in favor of traditional methods that prioritize environmental sustainability and soil health.

Beyond its agricultural heritage, Viñales is also a haven for nature lovers and outdoor enthusiasts, with a wealth of hiking, horseback riding, and rock climbing opportunities available in the surrounding countryside. The Viñales Valley is crisscrossed by a network of scenic trails that wind through lush forests, past cascading waterfalls, and up to panoramic viewpoints, offering breathtaking vistas of the valley below.

For those interested in exploring the cultural heritage of Viñales, the town itself offers charming colonial architecture, lively markets, and a vibrant arts scene. Visitors can wander through the colorful streets, visit local artisan workshops, and sample traditional Cuban cuisine at the town's many restaurants and cafes.

Overall, Viñales offers a unique opportunity to experience the beauty and tranquility of rural Cuba, where nature and agriculture come together to create a landscape of unparalleled beauty and diversity. Whether exploring the verdant valleys, learning about traditional farming practices, or simply soaking up the natural beauty of the countryside, Viñales offers a truly unforgettable experience for travelers seeking to connect with the land and the culture of Cuba.

Bay of Pigs: History and Controversy

The Bay of Pigs, known as Bahía de Cochinos in Spanish, is a site steeped in history and controversy. Located on the southern coast of Cuba, the Bay of Pigs gained international notoriety in April 1961, when it became the scene of a failed invasion by Cuban exiles backed by the United States government.

The invasion, known as the Bay of Pigs Invasion or Playa Girón Invasion, was a pivotal moment in the Cold War, marking the height of tensions between the United States and Cuba during the early years of Fidel Castro's revolutionary government. The invasion was launched with the aim of overthrowing Castro's regime and installing a pro-American government in its place.

The Bay of Pigs Invasion began on April 17, 1961, when a force of around 1,400 Cuban exiles landed at Playa Girón and Playa Larga, two beaches on the eastern side of the Bay of Pigs. The invasion was met with fierce resistance from Cuban government forces, who were well-prepared and heavily armed.

Despite initial successes, the invasion quickly faltered, with the Cuban exiles becoming bogged down in heavy fighting and facing logistical and strategic challenges. The United States, which had provided support and training to the exiles, failed to provide the air cover and logistical support that had been promised, leading to the collapse of the invasion within three days.

The Bay of Pigs Invasion was a humiliating defeat for the United States and a propaganda victory for Fidel Castro's government, which portrayed the invasion as a heroic defense of Cuban sovereignty against imperialist aggression. The failed invasion also had far-reaching consequences for US-Cuba relations, solidifying Castro's grip on power and pushing Cuba further into the orbit of the Soviet Union.

In Cuba, the Bay of Pigs Invasion is remembered as a moment of national pride and defiance, symbolizing the resilience of the Cuban people in the face of foreign aggression. The Bay of Pigs itself has become a symbol of Cuban resistance and a pilgrimage site for Cuban revolutionaries and supporters of the Castro government.

Despite the passage of time, the Bay of Pigs Invasion remains a source of controversy and debate, with differing interpretations of its causes, consequences, and significance. For some, it is a cautionary tale about the dangers of foreign intervention and imperialist aggression, while for others, it is a reminder of the enduring struggle for freedom and self-determination in the face of tyranny and oppression.

Che Guevara: Icon of Revolution

Che Guevara, born Ernesto Guevara de la Serna on June 14, 1928, in Rosario, Argentina, is perhaps one of the most iconic figures of the 20th century. He emerged as a symbol of revolution, rebellion, and social justice, leaving an indelible mark on the history of Latin America and the world.

Guevara's journey towards becoming an icon of revolution began with his early travels through South America, where he witnessed firsthand the poverty, inequality, and social injustice that plagued the region. These experiences deeply influenced Guevara's political beliefs and fueled his commitment to social change and revolution.

In 1953, Guevara joined Fidel Castro's revolutionary movement in Cuba, which sought to overthrow the dictatorship of Fulgencio Batista and establish a socialist government. Guevara played a key role in the Cuban Revolution, serving as a military strategist, guerrilla fighter, and trusted advisor to Castro.

Guevara's role in the Cuban Revolution catapulted him to international fame and cemented his reputation as a symbol of revolutionary fervor and defiance against imperialism. His iconic image, captured in Alberto Korda's famous photograph "Guerrillero Heroico," became synonymous with the struggle for liberation and social justice around the world.

After the Cuban Revolution, Guevara continued to advocate for revolutionary change and socialist ideals, traveling to Africa and Latin America to support revolutionary movements in countries such as Congo and Bolivia. In Bolivia, Guevara attempted to replicate the success of the Cuban Revolution by leading a guerrilla insurgency against the government of President René Barrientos. However, the insurgency ultimately failed, and Guevara was captured and executed by Bolivian government forces on October 9, 1967.

Despite his death, Guevara's legacy lives on, inspiring generations of activists, revolutionaries, and social movements to fight for a better world. His writings, including "The Motorcycle Diaries" and "Guerrilla Warfare," continue to be studied and revered by scholars and revolutionaries alike, offering insights into his revolutionary ideology and vision for a more just and equitable society.

Today, Che Guevara remains a potent symbol of resistance and revolution, his image adorning t-shirts, posters, and murals around the world. While opinions about Guevara vary widely, from hero to villain, there is no denying his lasting impact on the course of history and his enduring legacy as an icon of revolution.

Afro-Cuban Culture: Rhythms and Traditions

Afro-Cuban culture is a vibrant and dynamic fusion of African, Spanish, and indigenous influences, reflecting the rich cultural heritage of the African diaspora in Cuba. From music and dance to religion and cuisine, Afro-Cuban culture permeates every aspect of Cuban society, shaping its identity and contributing to its unique cultural landscape.

At the heart of Afro-Cuban culture are its rhythmic traditions, which draw heavily from African musical styles such as rumba, son, and Afro-Cuban jazz. These rhythms, characterized by syncopated beats, complex polyrhythms, and call-and-response patterns, form the foundation of Cuban music and are a central feature of Afro-Cuban cultural expression.

One of the most iconic Afro-Cuban musical genres is rumba, a lively and improvisational style of music and dance that originated in the neighborhoods of Havana and Matanzas. Rumba is performed with a combination of drums, percussion instruments, and vocals, with dancers moving to the rhythm of the music in intricate and expressive ways.

Afro-Cuban religious traditions, such as Santería and Palo Monte, also play a significant role in

54

shaping the cultural landscape of Cuba. These religions, which synthesize African spiritual beliefs with Catholicism, are practiced by millions of Cubans and have a profound influence on daily life, rituals, and customs.

Santería, in particular, is known for its elaborate ceremonies, colorful rituals, and devotion to the Orishas, or deities, which are believed to govern various aspects of human existence. Palo Monte, on the other hand, emphasizes the worship of nature spirits and ancestral spirits, with practitioners seeking guidance and protection from these spiritual forces. In addition to music, dance, and religion, Afro-Cuban culture is also celebrated through its vibrant culinary traditions, which blend African, Spanish, and indigenous ingredients and flavors. Dishes such as congri, a combination of rice and black beans, and ropa vieja, a hearty stew made with shredded beef, are staples of Afro-Cuban cuisine, reflecting the influence of African culinary traditions on Cuban gastronomy.

Overall, Afro-Cuban culture is a testament to the resilience, creativity, and spirit of the African diaspora in Cuba, enriching the country's cultural tapestry and contributing to its global reputation as a vibrant and dynamic cultural hub. Through its music, dance, religion, and cuisine, Afro-Cuban culture continues to inspire and captivate audiences around the world, celebrating the diversity and richness of Cuban identity.

Cuban Music: Salsa, Son, and Rumba

Cuban music is a vibrant tapestry woven with diverse rhythms, melodies, and influences, reflecting the island's rich cultural heritage and history. At its core are genres such as salsa, son, and rumba, each with its own unique characteristics and origins.

Salsa, often referred to as the "heartbeat of Cuba," is a dynamic and infectious musical genre that emerged in the late 1960s and early 1970s as a fusion of Cuban son, Puerto Rican bomba and plena, and American jazz and soul. Characterized by its syncopated rhythms, Afro-Cuban percussion, and brass instrumentation, salsa quickly gained popularity throughout Latin America and the world, becoming a global phenomenon that continues to thrive today.

Son, considered the cornerstone of Cuban music, traces its roots back to the late 19th century, when African and Spanish musical traditions merged in the urban centers of eastern Cuba. Derived from the Spanish word for "sound" or "tune," son is characterized by its infectious rhythms, melodic guitar lines, and call-and-response vocals. It laid the groundwork for many other Cuban musical styles, including salsa, mambo, and cha-cha-chá, and remains an integral part of the island's musical identity.

Rumba, another quintessentially Cuban genre, is a vibrant and energetic style of music and dance that originated in the neighborhoods of Havana and Matanzas during the late 19th and early 20th centuries. Rooted in African religious and cultural traditions, rumba is characterized by its driving rhythms, intricate percussion, and expressive dance movements. It encompasses several subgenres, including guaguancó, yambú, and columbia, each with its own distinct rhythms and choreography.

In addition to salsa, son, and rumba, Cuban music is also known for its rich array of other musical styles and genres, including mambo, cha-cha-chá, bolero, and danzón, among others. These genres draw from a diverse range of influences, including African, Spanish, French, and American musical traditions, resulting in a dynamic and eclectic musical landscape that reflects the cultural diversity of Cuba.

Throughout its history, Cuban music has played a central role in shaping the identity and culture of the island, serving as a source of pride, expression, and resistance in the face of social and political challenges. From the vibrant streets of Havana to the remote countryside villages, music permeates every aspect of Cuban life, bringing people together and celebrating the rich tapestry of Cuban identity and heritage.

Cuban Art: From Colonial to Contemporary

Cuban art is a dynamic and diverse expression of the island's cultural heritage, encompassing a wide range of styles, mediums, and influences from colonial times to the present day. The roots of Cuban art can be traced back to the colonial period when European artists introduced academic traditions and techniques to the island, resulting in a flourishing of religious and portrait painting in churches and aristocratic homes.

During the 19th century, Cuban art underwent a period of transformation as artists began to explore national identity and cultural heritage in their work. The landscape became a popular subject, with artists such as Esteban Chartrand and Miguel Melero capturing the beauty of the Cuban countryside in their paintings. At the same time, Afro-Cuban themes and imagery began to emerge in art, reflecting the island's rich African heritage and cultural diversity.

The early 20th century saw the rise of modernism in Cuban art, with artists such as Amelia Peláez, Wifredo Lam, and René Portocarrero blending European modernist influences with Afro-Cuban motifs and symbolism. These artists embraced abstraction, cubism, and surrealism, creating bold and

58

expressive works that challenged traditional notions of Cuban art and identity.

The Cuban Revolution of 1959 marked a turning point in the history of Cuban art, with the government embracing art as a tool for social and political change. The establishment of institutions such as the National Art Schools and the Cuban Institute of Cinematographic Art and Industry (ICAIC) provided artists with resources and support to explore new artistic directions and engage with revolutionary themes and ideologies.

During the 1960s and 1970s, socialist realism became the dominant style in Cuban art, with artists such as Raúl Martínez and Alfredo Sosabravo creating propaganda posters and murals that celebrated the achievements of the revolution and promoted socialist values. At the same time, artists such as Antonia Eiriz and Tomás Sánchez used their work to critique social and political issues and advocate for artistic freedom and individual expression.

Since the 1990s, Cuban art has experienced a resurgence of creativity and experimentation, with artists embracing a wide range of styles, mediums, and themes. The emergence of the "Generation of the 80s," a group of young artists who came of age during the economic hardships

59

of the Special Period, brought new energy and diversity to Cuban art, exploring themes such as globalization, identity, and cultural exchange in their work.

Today, Cuban art continues to evolve and thrive, with artists drawing inspiration from the island's rich cultural heritage, political history, and social realities. From traditional painting and sculpture to experimental installations and multimedia projects, Cuban art reflects the complexity and diversity of Cuban society, offering a window into the past, present, and future of this vibrant and dynamic island nation.

Cuban Literature: Voices of Resilience

Cuban literature is a testament to the resilience, creativity, and spirit of the Cuban people, capturing the essence of the island's history, culture, and identity through the written word. From the early colonial period to the present day, Cuban writers have used literature as a means of expression, protest, and celebration, offering insights into the complexities of Cuban society and the human experience.

The roots of Cuban literature can be traced back to the colonial period when Spanish explorers and settlers first arrived on the island. Early Cuban literature was characterized by religious and historical texts, often written in Spanish and focused on themes such as conquest, colonization, and Catholicism. One of the earliest examples of Cuban literature is "La historia verdadera de la conquista de la Nueva España" (The True History of the Conquest of New Spain) by Bernal Díaz del Castillo, a firsthand account of the Spanish conquest of Mexico.

During the 19th century, Cuban literature underwent a period of transformation as writers began to explore themes of national identity, independence, and social justice in their work.

Figures such as José Martí, often considered the father of Cuban literature, played a pivotal role in shaping the island's literary landscape, advocating for independence from Spanish colonial rule through poetry, essays, and political activism.

The early 20th century saw the emergence of the "modernista" movement in Cuban literature, characterized by its emphasis on aestheticism, symbolism, and formal experimentation. Writers such as Julián del Casal and José Lezama Lima explored themes of beauty, desire, and existential angst in their poetry and prose, laying the groundwork for the development of Cuban modernism.

The Cuban Revolution of 1959 brought about significant changes in Cuban literature, with writers grappling with the social, political, and cultural upheaval of the revolutionary period. The government's emphasis on socialist realism and revolutionary themes in literature led to the emergence of a new generation of writers, such as Alejo Carpentier, Guillermo Cabrera Infante, and Reinaldo Arenas, who explored themes of identity, exile, and dissent in their work.

Despite censorship and repression, Cuban literature continued to thrive in the latter half of the 20th century, with writers such as Pedro Juan

Gutiérrez, Zoé Valdés, and Leonardo Padura pushing the boundaries of literary expression and experimentation. Their work, which often explores the gritty realities of contemporary Cuban life, has earned international acclaim and recognition, cementing their place in the pantheon of Cuban literature.

Today, Cuban literature remains a vibrant and dynamic field, with writers continuing to explore a wide range of themes, styles, and genres. From poetry and fiction to memoirs and essays, Cuban writers continue to offer unique perspectives on the human condition, providing a voice for the marginalized, the oppressed, and the disenfranchised in Cuban society. Through their words, Cuban writers continue to inspire, challenge, and provoke, ensuring that the voices of resilience are heard loud and clear in the literary landscape of Cuba.

Religion in Cuba: Syncretism and Spirituality

Religion in Cuba is a complex and multifaceted phenomenon, shaped by centuries of cultural exchange, migration, and colonialism. At its core is a unique blend of African, Spanish, and indigenous religious traditions, resulting in a syncretic and diverse spiritual landscape that reflects the island's rich cultural heritage.

One of the most prominent religious practices in Cuba is Santería, a syncretic religion that blends elements of Yoruba religion brought by African slaves with Catholicism introduced by Spanish colonizers. Santería, which means "the way of the saints," centers around the worship of Orishas, or deities, who are believed to govern various aspects of human existence. Practitioners of Santería often participate in elaborate ceremonies and rituals, including drumming, dancing, and animal sacrifice, to honor and appease the Orishas and seek their blessings and protection.

In addition to Santería, other Afro-Cuban religions such as Palo Monte and Abakuá are also practiced in Cuba, each with its own distinct beliefs, rituals, and traditions. Palo Monte, also known as "Las Reglas de Congo," emphasizes the worship of nature spirits and ancestral spirits, while Abakuá, a secretive male-only society, honors the spirit of the leopard and traces its origins to West Africa.

Alongside Afro-Cuban religions, Catholicism remains a dominant force in Cuban religious life, with a majority of the population identifying as Catholic. Catholicism in Cuba is characterized by a unique blend of indigenous and African religious beliefs and practices, resulting in a syncretic form of Catholicism that incorporates elements of Santería and other Afro-Cuban religions. Popular Catholic devotions such as the cult of the Virgin of Charity of El Cobre, the patron saint of Cuba, are deeply ingrained in Cuban culture and continue to attract devotees from all walks of life.

In recent years, there has been a resurgence of interest in Afro-Cuban religions and spirituality, fueled in part by the relaxation of government restrictions on religious practices and the increasing visibility of Afro-Cuban cultural heritage. Many Cubans, particularly younger generations, are rediscovering their roots and embracing Afro-Cuban religious traditions as a source of identity, community, and empowerment.

Despite the enduring influence of Afro-Cuban religions and Catholicism, Cuba is also home to a diverse array of other religious traditions, including Protestantism, Judaism, and Islam, among others. These religious communities coexist peacefully with one another, contributing to the cultural and religious tapestry of the island and reflecting Cuba's long history of religious pluralism and tolerance.

Overall, religion in Cuba is a dynamic and ever-evolving phenomenon, deeply intertwined with the island's history, culture, and identity. Whether through Afro-Cuban rituals, Catholic devotions, or other religious practices, spirituality continues to play a central role in the lives of many Cubans, providing a source of comfort, community, and connection in an ever-changing world.

Education and Healthcare: Achievements and Challenges

Education and healthcare in Cuba are often lauded as significant achievements of the revolutionary government, showcasing the island's commitment to social welfare and equality. Since the early days of the revolution, education and healthcare have been top priorities, with the government implementing policies aimed at providing free and universal access to both services for all Cuban citizens.

In terms of education, Cuba boasts one of the highest literacy rates in the world, with nearly 100% of the population being literate. Education is compulsory for children up to the ninth grade, and the government provides free education from preschool through university. Cuban schools emphasize academic rigor, with a focus on critical thinking, creativity, and social responsibility. The country's educational system has produced high levels of literacy, numeracy, and scientific knowledge among its citizens, contributing to Cuba's reputation as a center of intellectual and academic excellence.

In addition to formal education, Cuba also places a strong emphasis on vocational training and technical education, providing opportunities for students to pursue careers in fields such as

67

healthcare, engineering, agriculture, and the arts. Technical and vocational schools offer specialized training programs that equip students with the skills and knowledge needed to succeed in their chosen professions, helping to meet the needs of the labor market and promote economic development.

In the healthcare sector, Cuba is known for its comprehensive and universal healthcare system, which provides free medical care to all Cuban citizens. The country boasts one of the highest doctor-to-patient ratios in the world, with thousands of doctors and healthcare professionals serving in clinics, hospitals, and community health centers across the island. Cuban healthcare is based on a primary care model, with an emphasis on preventive medicine, community health promotion, and early intervention. The government invests heavily in healthcare infrastructure, medical research, and pharmaceutical development, ensuring access to essential medicines, vaccines, and medical technologies for all Cuban citizens.

Despite these achievements, Cuba's education and healthcare systems face significant challenges, including limited resources, infrastructure constraints, and economic hardships exacerbated by decades of US embargo and isolation. Shortages of essential supplies, equipment, and medications are common in Cuban hospitals and clinics, leading to difficulties in providing high-quality care to patients. Additionally, brain drain and emigration of skilled professionals have posed challenges to the sustainability of Cuba's healthcare system, with many doctors and nurses leaving the country in search of better opportunities abroad.

Overall, education and healthcare are foundational pillars of Cuban society, reflecting the government's commitment to social equity, human development, and the well-being of its citizens. Despite facing challenges, Cuba's achievements in these areas serve as a testament to the resilience, ingenuity, and resourcefulness of the Cuban people, who continue to strive for excellence and progress in the face of adversity.

Cuban Sports: Baseball and Beyond

Cuban sports, particularly baseball, hold a special place in the hearts of the Cuban people, serving as a source of national pride, identity, and unity. Baseball is often referred to as the "national pastime" of Cuba, with a long and storied history that dates back to the 19th century when the sport was introduced to the island by American sailors and immigrants. Since then, baseball has become deeply ingrained in Cuban culture, with millions of Cubans playing and following the sport with passion and enthusiasm.

Cuba has a rich tradition of producing world-class baseball players, many of whom have gone on to achieve success in Major League Baseball (MLB) and other professional leagues around the world. Players such as Tony Pérez, Luis Tiant, and Tony Oliva are among the most famous Cuban-born players to have made their mark on the international stage, earning accolades and recognition for their talent and skill.

In addition to baseball, Cuba excels in a variety of other sports, including boxing, track and field, volleyball, and basketball. Cuban athletes have achieved remarkable success in international competitions, winning numerous Olympic medals and world championships across a range of sports. The Cuban boxing team, in particular, is renowned for its dominance in the sport, producing legendary fighters such as Teófilo Stevenson and Félix Savón, who both won multiple Olympic gold medals.

Despite facing economic hardships and limited resources, Cuba continues to invest in sports development and infrastructure, providing opportunities for young athletes to pursue their dreams and excel in their chosen disciplines. The country's sports schools and academies offer training programs and support to aspiring athletes, nurturing talent and fostering a culture of excellence and achievement.

In recent years, Cuba has also made efforts to expand its sports diplomacy efforts, hosting international sporting events such as the Pan American Games and the Caribbean Series, which bring together athletes and teams from across the region and around the world. These events not only showcase Cuba's athletic prowess but also promote friendship, cooperation, and cultural exchange among nations.

Beyond the realm of traditional sports, Cuba is also known for its passion for dance, particularly salsa and rumba, which are celebrated and practiced by people of all ages and backgrounds. Dance plays a central role in Cuban culture, serving as a form of expression, social interaction, and artistic creativity. Cuban dancers and choreographers have gained international acclaim for their talent and innovation, contributing to the global popularity of Latin dance and music.

Overall, Cuban sports are a reflection of the island's vibrant culture, resilience, and spirit of competition. Whether on the baseball diamond, in the boxing ring, or on the dance floor, Cuban athletes and performers continue to inspire and captivate audiences around the world, showcasing the talent, passion, and determination of the Cuban people.

Cuban Festivals: Carnivals and Celebrations

Cuban festivals are vibrant and colorful celebrations that showcase the island's rich cultural heritage and diverse traditions. From carnivals to religious fiestas, Cuban festivals offer a unique opportunity to experience the music, dance, and food of this dynamic Caribbean nation.

One of the most famous Cuban festivals is the Havana Carnival, held annually in the capital city of Havana. This week-long celebration features parades, street performances, and live music, with participants donning elaborate costumes and masks as they dance through the streets of Old Havana. The Havana Carnival dates back to the colonial era and has its roots in African, Spanish, and indigenous traditions, making it a vibrant and multicultural event that attracts visitors from around the world.

Another popular Cuban festival is the Santiago de Cuba Carnival, held in the eastern city of Santiago de Cuba. Known as the "Carnival of the Caribbean," this lively event features colorful floats, traditional music, and dance competitions, including the famous conga, a high-energy dance procession that winds its way through the streets of Santiago. The Santiago de Cuba Carnival is a celebration of Afro-Cuban culture and heritage, with participants paying homage to the island's African roots through music, dance, and ritual.

Religious festivals also play a significant role in Cuban culture, with events such as the Feast of San Lázaro and the Feast of the Virgin of Charity of El Cobre drawing thousands of pilgrims and worshippers each year. The Feast of San Lázaro, held in the town of El Rincón, is dedicated to the Catholic saint of healing and features processions, prayers, and offerings to the saint, while the Feast of the Virgin of Charity of El Cobre, Cuba's patron saint, is celebrated with masses, processions, and cultural events throughout the island.

In addition to traditional festivals, Cuba also hosts a variety of music and dance festivals throughout the year, including the International Jazz Plaza Festival, the International Ballet Festival of Havana, and the Havana World Music Festival, which showcase the talents of Cuban and international artists across a range of genres and styles.

Overall, Cuban festivals are a celebration of life, culture, and community, bringing people together to share in the joy and vibrancy of Cuban traditions. Whether you're dancing in the streets of Havana, marveling at the colorful costumes of the Santiago de Cuba Carnival, or participating in the religious rituals of San Lázaro, Cuban festivals offer an unforgettable experience that captures the spirit and essence of this vibrant Caribbean nation.

Cuban Dance: From Mambo to Cha-Cha-Cha

Cuban dance is a vibrant and integral part of the island's cultural identity, reflecting the diverse influences and traditions that have shaped Cuban society over the centuries. From the rhythmic beats of the conga to the sultry moves of the mambo, Cuban dance embodies the spirit of joy, passion, and celebration that defines the Cuban people.

One of the most iconic Cuban dances is the mambo, which originated in the 1940s and quickly became a global sensation. Combining elements of Afro-Cuban rhythms with jazz and swing influences, the mambo is characterized by its energetic movements, syncopated rhythms, and infectious groove. The mambo gained popularity in nightclubs and dance halls across Cuba and the United States, with famous musicians such as Pérez Prado and Tito Puente popularizing the dance and its accompanying music.

Another popular Cuban dance is the cha-cha-cha, which emerged in the 1950s as a variation of the mambo. Known for its distinctive syncopated rhythm and playful footwork, the cha-cha-cha quickly became a favorite among dancers worldwide, thanks in part to its catchy melodies and infectious beats. The cha-cha-cha is often performed to a variety of Cuban music styles, including son, mambo, and bolero, and continues to be a staple of Latin dance clubs and competitions around the world.

In addition to the mambo and cha-cha-cha, Cuba is also known for its vibrant folkloric dances, which draw inspiration from African, Spanish, and indigenous traditions. One such dance is the rumba, a sensual and rhythmic dance that originated in the Afro-Cuban communities of Havana and Matanzas. The rumba is characterized by its improvisational movements, intricate footwork, and call-and-response vocals, with dancers expressing emotions such as love, passion, and defiance through their movements.

Cuban dance is not only a form of entertainment but also a means of cultural expression and social cohesion. Dance plays a central role in Cuban life, with people of all ages and backgrounds coming together to dance at parties, festivals, and celebrations. Whether it's the elegant movements of the salsa, the lively steps of the conga, or the passionate embraces of the tango, Cuban dance continues to captivate and inspire dancers and audiences around the world, showcasing the beauty, diversity, and vitality of Cuban culture.

Cuban Cigars: Tradition and Craftsmanship

Cuban cigars are renowned worldwide for their exceptional quality, craftsmanship, and rich flavor profiles, making them a symbol of luxury and prestige. Dating back centuries, the tradition of cigar-making in Cuba has been passed down through generations, with skilled artisans known as "torcedores" meticulously hand-rolling each cigar to perfection.

One of the key factors contributing to the exceptional quality of Cuban cigars is the country's unique climate and soil conditions. Cuba's warm, humid climate, coupled with its fertile soil rich in minerals, provides the ideal environment for growing tobacco, resulting in leaves that are prized for their flavor, aroma, and texture. The Vuelta Abajo region in the Pinar del Río province is particularly renowned for producing some of the finest tobacco in the world, known as "tabaco negro" or "black tobacco."

Cuban cigars are made from three types of tobacco leaves: filler, binder, and wrapper. The filler, which forms the body of the cigar, is made from a blend of different tobacco leaves, each selected for its unique flavor characteristics. The binder, a single leaf, is used to hold the filler together and provide structure to the cigar. Finally, the wrapper, often the most prized and carefully selected leaf, is used to encase the cigar, imparting flavor, aroma, and visual appeal.

The process of making Cuban cigars is a labor-intensive and highly skilled craft that requires years of training and experience. Each step, from selecting the tobacco leaves to rolling and finishing the cigars, is done by hand, with meticulous attention to detail and quality control. Torcedores undergo rigorous apprenticeships under master cigar-makers, learning the art and techniques of cigar rolling before they are allowed to work independently.

Cuban cigars are known for their distinct flavor profiles, which can vary depending on factors such as the type of tobacco used, the size and shape of the cigar, and the aging process. Common flavor notes found in Cuban cigars include earthy, woody, spicy, and floral tones, with each cigar offering a unique and memorable smoking experience.

In addition to their exceptional quality, Cuban cigars also hold a special place in popular culture and history, with aficionados and collectors around the world coveting rare and limited-edition releases. Cuban cigars have been smoked by some of the world's most influential figures, from politicians and celebrities to artists and intellectuals, further adding to their mystique and allure.

Despite their popularity, Cuban cigars face challenges in the global market, including competition from other cigar-producing countries and restrictions on trade imposed by the US embargo. Nevertheless, Cuban cigars remain highly sought after by connoisseurs and enthusiasts alike, continuing to uphold the tradition of excellence and craftsmanship that has made them synonymous with luxury and indulgence.

Cuban Rum: Spirit of the Caribbean

Cuban rum holds a special place in the world of spirits, renowned for its rich history, distinctive flavor, and cultural significance. Dating back centuries, rum production in Cuba has been intertwined with the island's colonial past, sugarcane industry, and vibrant culture, making it a symbol of Cuban identity and hospitality.

The origins of rum production in Cuba can be traced back to the early days of Spanish colonization, when sugarcane was introduced to the island and quickly became a primary crop. With an abundance of sugarcane available, Cuban farmers began distilling rum as a way to utilize excess molasses, a byproduct of sugar production. These early rums were crude and unrefined but laid the foundation for the development of Cuba's rum industry.

Over time, Cuban rum production evolved and refined, with distillers experimenting with different fermentation and distillation techniques to create spirits of superior quality and complexity. By the 19th century, Cuban rum had gained recognition and popularity both domestically and internationally, with brands such as Havana Club and Bacardi becoming household names around the world. Cuban rum is typically made using a blend of sugarcane juice and molasses, which are fermented, distilled, and aged in oak barrels to develop their distinctive flavors and aromas. The aging process plays a crucial role in the development of Cuban rum, with rums aged for varying lengths of time to achieve different flavor profiles. Cuban rum is known for its smoothness, balance, and depth of flavor, with notes of tropical fruits, spices, and oak imparted by the aging process. In addition to its quality and craftsmanship, Cuban rum is also celebrated for its role in Cuban culture and social life. Rum plays a central role in traditional Cuban cocktails such as the mojito, daiquiri, and Cuba Libre, which are enjoyed by locals and visitors alike at bars, restaurants, and social gatherings across the island. Rum is also used in culinary dishes and desserts, adding depth and richness to traditional Cuban cuisine. Despite its popularity, Cuban rum has faced challenges in recent years, including disruptions to production caused by political unrest and economic hardship. The US embargo on Cuban goods has also limited the availability of Cuban rum in the international market, making it a rare and sought-after commodity for rum enthusiasts and collectors around the world.

Nevertheless, Cuban rum continues to be cherished and celebrated by those who appreciate its rich history, exceptional quality, and cultural significance. Whether sipped neat, mixed into a cocktail, or enjoyed as part of a culinary experience, Cuban rum remains a timeless symbol of the spirit and resilience of the Caribbean.

Exploring Cuba: Tips for Travelers

Exploring Cuba offers travelers a unique and immersive experience, with its rich history, vibrant culture, and stunning landscapes waiting to be discovered. Whether you're strolling through the colorful streets of Havana, hiking in the lush Viñales Valley, or relaxing on the pristine beaches of Varadero, Cuba has something to offer for every type of traveler.

Before embarking on your journey to Cuba, it's essential to do your research and plan ahead. While Cuba is a safe destination overall, it's essential to be aware of any travel advisories or restrictions that may be in place, as well as the current political and social climate. Additionally, US citizens should be aware of the restrictions imposed by the US government on travel to Cuba, including limitations on spending and transactions while in the country.

When it comes to getting around in Cuba, there are several options available to travelers. Public transportation, including buses and taxis, is readily available in major cities and tourist areas, but may be less reliable in more remote areas. Renting a car is also an option for those who prefer more flexibility and independence, but it's essential to be aware of the condition of the roads and driving regulations in Cuba.

Accommodation options in Cuba range from luxury resorts and boutique hotels to casa particulares, or private homestays. Staying in a casa particular is a great way to experience Cuban hospitality and connect with local people, while also supporting small businesses and families. It's a good idea to book accommodation in advance, especially during peak tourist seasons, to ensure availability.

When it comes to money in Cuba, it's important to be prepared. The official currency in Cuba is the Cuban peso (CUP), but most tourists use the Cuban convertible peso (CUC), which is pegged to the US dollar. It's recommended to bring cash with you to exchange for CUC upon arrival, as credit and debit cards issued by US banks are often not accepted in Cuba due to the US embargo.

Cuba is a country rich in culture and history, with a wealth of attractions and activities to explore. From UNESCO World Heritage sites such as Old Havana and Trinidad to natural wonders like the Zapata Swamp and Sierra Maestra mountains, there's no shortage of things to see and do in Cuba. Whether you're interested in history, art, music, or outdoor adventure, Cuba offers something for everyone.

One of the highlights of any trip to Cuba is experiencing the local cuisine. Cuban food is a delicious blend of Spanish, African, and Caribbean flavors, with dishes such as arroz con pollo, ropa vieja, and tostones being popular favorites. Be sure to try local specialties like Cuban sandwiches, black beans and rice, and fresh seafood, as well as refreshing drinks like mojitos and piña coladas.

Overall, exploring Cuba is a rewarding and unforgettable experience, offering travelers the opportunity to immerse themselves in a vibrant culture, connect with friendly locals, and create lasting memories. By following these tips and being respectful of local customs and traditions, you can make the most of your time in this beautiful and fascinating country.

Havana Vieja: Walking Through History

Havana Vieja, or Old Havana, is a captivating neighborhood that serves as the heart and soul of Cuba's capital city. Stepping into Havana Vieja feels like stepping back in time, with its cobblestone streets, colonial architecture, and historic landmarks transporting visitors to a bygone era.

Founded by the Spanish in 1519, Havana Vieja is one of the oldest and most well-preserved colonial cities in the Americas. Its layout, characterized by narrow streets and picturesque plazas, reflects its Spanish colonial heritage, with buildings dating back to the 16th and 17th centuries lining its streets. Many of these buildings have been meticulously restored and renovated, preserving their original charm and architectural features.

Walking through Havana Vieja is like taking a journey through history, with each street and square telling a story of the city's past. One of the most iconic landmarks in Havana Vieja is the Plaza de la Catedral, home to the stunning Havana Cathedral. Built in the 18th century, the cathedral is a masterpiece of baroque architecture, with its ornate facade and twin bell towers dominating the skyline.

Another must-visit attraction in Havana Vieja is the Plaza de Armas, the oldest square in the city and a hub of activity since colonial times. Surrounded by historic buildings and lined with shady trees, the Plaza de Armas is the perfect place to soak up the atmosphere of Old Havana, with street vendors selling books, artwork, and souvenirs, and locals and tourists alike gathering to relax and enjoy the ambiance.

Havana Vieja is also home to a wealth of museums, galleries, and cultural institutions, where visitors can learn about Cuba's rich history and heritage. The Museo de la Revolución, housed in the former Presidential Palace, offers insight into Cuba's revolutionary past, while the Museo Nacional de Bellas Artes showcases the country's vibrant artistic traditions.

In addition to its historic and cultural attractions, Havana Vieja is also a vibrant and lively neighborhood, with bustling markets, lively music, and delicious cuisine waiting to be discovered around every corner. From sipping mojitos in a rooftop bar to dancing salsa in a local club, there's no shortage of ways to experience the vibrant energy and spirit of Havana Vieja.

Overall, walking through Havana Vieja is an unforgettable experience, offering travelers the opportunity to immerse themselves in the history, culture, and beauty of one of the world's most enchanting cities. Whether you're exploring its historic landmarks, sampling its culinary delights, or simply soaking up the atmosphere, Havana Vieja is sure to leave a lasting impression on all who visit.

Malecón: The Soul of Havana

The Malecón is more than just a seawall; it's the beating heart of Havana, pulsating with life, culture, and history. Stretching for five miles along the city's coastline, the Malecón is a beloved gathering place for locals and visitors alike, offering stunning views of the sea and serving as a backdrop for countless moments of joy, reflection, and connection.

Constructed in the early 20th century, the Malecón was originally built to protect Havana from the ravages of the sea, but it quickly evolved into much more than a defensive barrier. Over the years, the Malecón has become an iconic symbol of Havana, embodying the spirit and resilience of the Cuban people. It's a place where generations of Habaneros have come to relax, socialize, and enjoy the simple pleasures of life.

Walking along the Malecón, you'll encounter a vibrant tapestry of sights and sounds, from fishermen casting their lines into the waves to musicians playing traditional Cuban music on street corners. It's a place where the rhythms of daily life blend seamlessly with the rhythms of the sea, creating a sense of harmony and connection that is uniquely Cuban.

One of the most iconic features of the Malecón is its eclectic mix of architectural styles, with grand colonial buildings standing side by side with sleek modernist structures. From the historic Hotel Nacional de Cuba to the imposing Castillo de los Tres Reyes del Morro, the Malecón is lined with architectural gems that reflect Cuba's rich and diverse cultural heritage.

But perhaps the most enduring legacy of the Malecón is its role as a gathering place for the Cuban people, a place where they come together to celebrate, protest, and simply be together. From impromptu street parties to political demonstrations, the Malecón has witnessed countless moments of triumph and tragedy, joy and sorrow, shaping the collective memory and identity of the Cuban nation.

Today, the Malecón remains as vibrant and vital as ever, attracting visitors from around the world who come to experience its unique blend of beauty, history, and culture. Whether you're strolling along its promenade at sunset, listening to the waves crashing against the seawall, or simply soaking up the atmosphere, the Malecón offers a glimpse into the soul of Havana, inviting you to become a part of its rich tapestry of life.

Old Towns of Trinidad and Cienfuegos: Time Capsules of Colonial Cuba

Trinidad and Cienfuegos are two of Cuba's most enchanting old towns, each offering a glimpse into the country's colonial past and preserving the architectural and cultural heritage of centuries gone by.

Trinidad, located on the southern coast of Cuba, is a UNESCO World Heritage site renowned for its well-preserved colonial architecture and cobblestone streets. Founded in the early 16th century by Spanish conquistadors, Trinidad quickly became one of Cuba's wealthiest cities, thanks to its booming sugar industry and strategic location on the Caribbean trade routes.

Walking through the streets of Trinidad feels like stepping back in time, with its colorful colonial buildings, ornate churches, and bustling plazas transporting visitors to the days of Spanish colonial rule. Highlights of Trinidad include the Plaza Mayor, the city's central square surrounded by elegant mansions and the iconic Palacio Cantero, now home to the Museo Histórico Municipal.

Just a short drive from Trinidad lies the picturesque town of Cienfuegos, often referred to as the "Pearl of the South" for its stunning waterfront setting and neoclassical architecture. Founded in the early 19th century by French settlers, Cienfuegos is known for its wide boulevards, manicured parks, and grand colonial buildings, which reflect its French and Spanish heritage.

The centerpiece of Cienfuegos is the Parque José Martí, a leafy plaza surrounded by historic buildings such as the Teatro Tomás Terry and the Palacio de Gobierno. The nearby Punta Gorda neighborhood, with its elegant mansions and waterfront promenade, offers a glimpse into Cienfuegos' affluent past as a hub of commerce and culture.

Both Trinidad and Cienfuegos offer visitors a wealth of attractions and activities to explore, from museums and art galleries to scenic overlooks and outdoor adventures. Whether you're wandering through Trinidad's artisan markets, exploring Cienfuegos' botanical gardens, or simply soaking up the atmosphere in one of the town's charming cafes, you're sure to be captivated by the timeless beauty and charm of these colonial Cuban treasures.

El Capitolio: Symbol of Cuban Republic

El Capitolio, or the National Capitol Building, stands as one of the most iconic landmarks in Havana, Cuba, symbolizing the country's rich history, cultural heritage, and political aspirations. Designed by Cuban architect Eugenio Rayneri Piedra and inspired by the United States Capitol in Washington, D.C., El Capitolio was constructed between 1926 and 1929 during the presidency of Gerardo Machado.

The building's neoclassical design features a massive dome towering over the city skyline, flanked by majestic columns and adorned with intricate sculptures and carvings. At the time of its completion, El Capitolio was the tallest building in Havana, a testament to Cuba's growing prosperity and ambitions on the world stage.

El Capitolio served as the seat of the Cuban government until the Cuban Revolution in 1959, when it was repurposed as the headquarters of the Academy of Sciences and the National Library of Science and Technology. Today, the building is a popular tourist attraction, drawing visitors from around the world who come to marvel at its grandeur and learn about its history.

One of the most impressive features of El Capitolio is its central hall, known as the Hall of the Lost Steps, which houses a replica of the Statue of the Republic, a bronze sculpture that was the third-largest indoor statue in the world at the time of its creation. The hall is adorned with marble floors, stained glass windows, and ornate chandeliers, creating a sense of grandeur and opulence befitting the building's status as a symbol of Cuban republicanism.

Surrounding the building is the Capitolio Square, a bustling plaza lined with palm trees, statues, and fountains, where locals and tourists alike gather to take in the sights and sounds of Havana. From the square, visitors can enjoy panoramic views of the city and the sea, with El Capitolio standing as a majestic backdrop against the Cuban sky.

Despite its historical significance and architectural beauty, El Capitolio has also been the subject of controversy and debate over the years. Some critics argue that the building's construction was a symbol of the corrupt and authoritarian regime of President Machado, while others see it as a symbol of Cuban nationalism and pride.

Regardless of its political connotations, El Capitolio remains a cherished symbol of Cuban identity and heritage, serving as a reminder of the country's rich history and its aspirations for the future. As visitors explore its halls and marvel at its architecture, they can't help but be captivated by the timeless beauty and grandeur of this iconic Cuban landmark.

Revolution Square: Political Heart of Havana

Revolution Square, or Plaza de la Revolución, is the political heart of Havana, Cuba, and serves as a focal point for political gatherings, demonstrations, and events. Covering an area of 11 hectares, it is one of the largest city squares in the world, capable of holding hundreds of thousands of people.

The square is dominated by two iconic structures: the José Martí Memorial and the Ministry of the Interior building. The José Martí Memorial is a towering white marble monument dedicated to the Cuban national hero, José Martí, who played a key role in the country's struggle for independence from Spain. Standing at over 350 feet tall, the memorial is topped by a 59-foot statue of Martí and offers panoramic views of Havana from its observation deck.

The Ministry of the Interior building is famous for its massive steel sculpture of Ernesto "Che" Guevara, the Argentine revolutionary who played a central role in the Cuban Revolution. The sculpture, which measures over 30 feet high, depicts Che with his trademark beret and stern expression, gazing out over the square with a sense of determination and resolve.

Revolution Square has been the site of many historic events in Cuban history, including speeches by Fidel Castro and other revolutionary leaders, as well as mass rallies and celebrations. It was here that Castro delivered his famous speeches, rallying the Cuban people and inspiring them to continue the fight for socialism and revolution.

Today, Revolution Square continues to play a central role in Cuban politics, serving as a venue for official ceremonies, political rallies, and cultural events. It is also a popular tourist attraction, drawing visitors from around the world who come to see its iconic monuments and learn about its significance in Cuban history.

But Revolution Square is more than just a political symbol; it is also a place of great cultural and social significance for the Cuban people. It is a gathering place where people come together to celebrate their shared values and ideals, to honor their heroes and martyrs, and to express their hopes and aspirations for the future.

As visitors stand in Revolution Square, surrounded by its towering monuments and sweeping vistas, they can't help but be struck by the sense of history and significance that permeates the air. It is a place where the past, present, and future converge, reminding us of the enduring power of revolution and the indomitable spirit of the Cuban people.

José Martí: National Hero and Poet

José Martí is a towering figure in Cuban history, revered as the national hero and poet who played a pivotal role in the country's struggle for independence from Spanish colonial rule. Born in Havana in 1853, Martí showed exceptional intellectual abilities from a young age, mastering multiple languages and demonstrating a keen interest in literature, politics, and social justice.

Martí's commitment to Cuban independence was evident from an early age, and he became involved in revolutionary activities while still a teenager. At the age of 16, he was arrested and sentenced to hard labor for his involvement in anti-colonial activities, setting the stage for a lifetime of resistance and defiance against Spanish rule.

Despite facing persecution and exile, Martí continued to advocate for Cuban independence through his writings and speeches, becoming a leading figure in the struggle for liberation. He founded several revolutionary organizations, including the Cuban Revolutionary Party, and worked tirelessly to mobilize support for the cause both at home and abroad.

Martí's literary contributions were equally significant, and he is widely regarded as one of the greatest poets and writers in Cuban literature. His works, which include poetry, essays, and journalism, are characterized by their eloquence, passion, and profound insights into the human condition.

One of Martí's most famous works is his essay "Our America" (Nuestra América), in which he articulates his vision for a united and independent Latin America free from foreign domination. In this seminal work, Martí argues for the importance of cultural and intellectual independence as a precursor to political liberation, laying the groundwork for the pan-Americanist movement that would emerge in the 20th century.

Martí's life was tragically cut short when he died in battle during the Cuban War of Independence in 1895, but his legacy lived on, inspiring generations of Cubans to continue the fight for freedom and justice. Today, Martí is celebrated as a national hero and martyr, with his image adorning currency, stamps, and monuments throughout Cuba.

His words continue to resonate with people around the world, serving as a source of inspiration for those who strive for a better and more just society. As Martí himself famously said, "Men are like the stars; some generate their own light while others reflect the brilliance they receive." In the case of José Martí, his brilliance shines brightly, illuminating the path toward freedom and dignity for all.

Hemingway's Cuba: Tracing the Author's Footsteps

Ernest Hemingway, one of the most celebrated American authors of the 20th century, found inspiration and solace in the vibrant and colorful landscapes of Cuba. Hemingway's connection to the island nation began in the 1930s when he first visited Cuba on a fishing trip and fell in love with its beauty and charm. He was drawn to the island's relaxed atmosphere, warm climate, and rich cultural heritage, and he would return to Cuba again and again over the years, eventually making it his home for more than two decades.

One of Hemingway's most famous haunts in Cuba was Finca Vigía, his beloved hilltop estate located just outside of Havana. Hemingway purchased the property in 1940 and spent many happy years there, writing some of his most famous works, including "For Whom the Bell Tolls" and "The Old Man and the Sea." Today, Finca Vigía is preserved as a museum, offering visitors a glimpse into Hemingway's life and legacy in Cuba.

Another iconic spot associated with Hemingway in Cuba is the El Floridita bar in Old Havana, known as the birthplace of the daiquiri cocktail. Hemingway was a regular at El Floridita, and he famously declared the bar's daiquiris to be the best in the world. A life-sized bronze statue of Hemingway now stands at the bar, commemorating his patronage and lasting influence on the establishment. In addition to Finca Vigía and El Floridita, Hemingway also frequented La Bodeguita del Medio, another historic bar in Old Havana famous for its mojitos and lively atmosphere. Like El Floridita, La Bodeguita del Medio has become a popular tourist destination, attracting visitors from around the world who come to sample its signature cocktails and soak up its vibrant ambiance.

Hemingway's presence in Cuba extended beyond the confines of Havana, as he often ventured into the countryside in search of adventure and inspiration. He was an avid sportsman and enjoyed fishing, hunting, and exploring the rugged terrain of the Cuban countryside. His experiences in Cuba influenced much of his writing, imbuing his works with a sense of authenticity and vitality that continues to resonate with readers today.

Despite his eventual departure from Cuba in the early 1960s, Hemingway's legacy lives on in the streets of Havana and the pages of his novels. His connection to the island remains a source of pride for many Cubans, who celebrate his life and work as part of their cultural heritage. For visitors to Cuba, tracing Hemingway's footsteps offers a unique opportunity to experience the island through the eyes of one of its most famous residents, immersing themselves in the sights, sounds, and flavors that inspired some of his greatest literary achievements.

Top Beaches in Cuba: Paradise Found

Cuba is renowned for its stunning beaches, boasting some of the most beautiful stretches of coastline in the Caribbean. With its pristine white sands, crystal-clear turquoise waters, and lush tropical surroundings, Cuba's beaches offer travelers a true paradise escape.

Varadero Beach is perhaps the most famous beach in Cuba, stretching for over 20 kilometers along the island's northern coast. With its powdery white sands and calm, shallow waters, Varadero is a favorite destination for sun-seekers and water sports enthusiasts alike. The beach is lined with resorts, hotels, and restaurants, offering visitors a range of amenities and activities to enjoy during their stay.

Another popular beach destination in Cuba is Playa Paraíso, located on the remote island of Cayo Largo del Sur. Accessible only by boat or plane, Playa Paraíso is a secluded oasis of tranquility, with its pristine sands and clear, turquoise waters. The beach is surrounded by mangrove forests and coral reefs, making it an ideal spot for snorkeling, diving, and exploring the underwater world.

For those seeking a more off-the-beaten-path beach experience, Playa Ancón near Trinidad is a hidden gem waiting to be discovered. Nestled along Cuba's southern coast, Playa Ancón boasts powdery white sands and calm, shallow waters perfect for swimming and sunbathing. The beach is fringed by swaying palm trees and offers stunning views of the Caribbean Sea, making it a picture-perfect destination for beach lovers.

Cuba's beaches are not only renowned for their natural beauty but also for their rich history and cultural significance. Many of the island's beaches are located near historic towns and cities, allowing visitors to combine beach relaxation with cultural exploration. For example, Playa Santa María near Havana offers visitors the chance to explore the capital's vibrant streets and colonial architecture before unwinding on its pristine shores.

Whether you're looking for a bustling beach resort or a secluded stretch of sand, Cuba offers a diverse range of beach experiences to suit every traveler's taste. From the iconic shores of Varadero to the remote beauty of Playa Paraíso, Cuba's beaches are sure to leave a lasting impression on anyone lucky enough to visit.

Viñales Valley: Exploring Cuba's Countryside

Nestled in the heart of western Cuba, the Viñales Valley is a picturesque region known for its stunning natural beauty, unique limestone formations, and rich agricultural heritage. Designated as a UNESCO World Heritage Site in 1999, the valley is a must-visit destination for travelers seeking to explore Cuba's countryside and experience its rural way of life.

One of the most striking features of the Viñales Valley is its mogotes, or towering limestone hills, which rise dramatically from the valley floor. These ancient formations, sculpted by millions of years of erosion, create a dramatic backdrop for the lush tobacco fields and traditional farming communities that dot the landscape.

Tobacco cultivation is a way of life in the Viñales Valley, and visitors have the opportunity to learn about the traditional methods of growing and harvesting tobacco from local farmers. Many tobacco farms in the valley offer guided tours, where visitors can see firsthand how tobacco leaves are grown, harvested, and processed to produce Cuba's famous cigars.

In addition to tobacco, the Viñales Valley is also known for its diverse agricultural production, including fruits, vegetables, and coffee. Visitors can explore the valley's vibrant markets and sample fresh, locally grown produce, or embark on guided hiking or horseback riding tours to discover the valley's hidden gems.

The town of Viñales serves as the gateway to the valley, offering a charming base for exploring the surrounding countryside. With its colorful colonial architecture, lively atmosphere, and welcoming locals, Viñales provides visitors with a taste of authentic Cuban culture and hospitality.

Beyond its natural beauty and agricultural heritage, the Viñales Valley is also home to several cultural and historical attractions. The Prehistoric Mural, a massive painting on the side of a mogote depicting the evolution of life on Earth, is a fascinating sight to behold and offers insight into the valley's geological history.

For outdoor enthusiasts, the Viñales Valley offers a wealth of recreational activities, including hiking, rock climbing, and cave exploration. The Cueva del Indio, a vast underground cave system, is a popular destination for cave tours and boat rides along its subterranean river.

Whether you're interested in exploring the valley's natural wonders, learning about its agricultural traditions, or simply soaking up its tranquil rural atmosphere, the Viñales Valley offers something for everyone. With its stunning landscapes, rich cultural heritage, and warm hospitality, it's no wonder that the Viñales Valley is considered one of Cuba's most beloved destinations.

Cuban Spanish: Language and Dialects

Cuban Spanish is a vibrant and distinctive dialect of the Spanish language, shaped by centuries of history, cultural influences, and regional variations. Like many other Spanish-speaking countries, Cuba has its own unique accent, vocabulary, and grammar rules that set it apart from other Spanish-speaking nations.

One of the most notable features of Cuban Spanish is its pronunciation, which is characterized by a soft and melodic rhythm. Cubans often speak with a sing-song cadence, elongating vowels and blending words together in a way that is both musical and expressive. This distinctive accent is influenced by the island's diverse cultural heritage, which includes Spanish, African, and indigenous influences.

In addition to its pronunciation, Cuban Spanish also features a rich vocabulary that reflects the island's history and cultural diversity. Cuban Spanish borrows words and phrases from various sources, including African languages, Taíno, and English, resulting in a colorful and dynamic linguistic landscape. For example, the word "guagua" is used in Cuba to refer to a bus, a term borrowed from the Taíno language.

Another unique aspect of Cuban Spanish is its use of slang and colloquial expressions, which add flavor and nuance to everyday communication. Cubans are known for their creative use of language, often employing humorous and playful expressions to convey their thoughts and emotions. From "chaval" (a term of endearment) to "chisme" (gossip), Cuban slang adds a layer of cultural richness to the language.

Despite its distinctive features, Cuban Spanish is also influenced by standard Spanish grammar and syntax, making it accessible to speakers of other Spanish dialects. However, there are some notable differences in grammar and usage, particularly in informal settings. For example, Cubans often use the informal pronoun "tú" instead of the formal "usted" when addressing friends and family members.

Regional variations in Cuban Spanish also exist, with differences in pronunciation, vocabulary, and grammar depending on the region of the country. For example, the Spanish spoken in Havana may differ from that spoken in Santiago de Cuba or Pinar del Río, reflecting the diverse cultural influences and historical developments of each region.

Overall, Cuban Spanish is a dynamic and expressive dialect that reflects the island's rich cultural heritage and linguistic diversity. Whether you're exploring the streets of Havana or chatting with locals in the countryside, the language of Cuba offers a fascinating window into the island's vibrant culture and history.

Cuban Proverbs: Insights into Cuban Culture

Cuban proverbs are like tiny capsules of wisdom, offering insights into the island's rich culture, history, and way of life. Passed down through generations, these sayings encapsulate the collective knowledge and experiences of the Cuban people, providing valuable lessons and guidance for navigating life's challenges and triumphs.

One of the most famous Cuban proverbs is "El que madruga, Dios lo ayuda," which translates to "The early bird catches the worm." This proverb reflects the value placed on hard work, initiative, and seizing opportunities in Cuban culture. It emphasizes the importance of being proactive and diligent in pursuing one's goals, echoing the island's strong work ethic and entrepreneurial spirit.

Another popular Cuban proverb is "No hay mal que por bien no venga," meaning "Every cloud has a silver lining." This proverb speaks to the resilience and optimism of the Cuban people, highlighting their ability to find hope and positivity in even the most challenging situations. It reflects a belief in the power of perseverance and the inherent goodness of life, despite its inevitable ups and downs.

Cuban proverbs often draw upon themes of family, community, and solidarity, reflecting the close-knit nature of Cuban society. For example, the saying "La familia es lo primero," meaning "Family comes first," underscores the importance of familial bonds and mutual support in Cuban culture. It emphasizes the idea that family is the cornerstone of society, providing strength, love, and protection in times of need.

In addition to offering practical advice and moral guidance, Cuban proverbs also serve as a means of cultural expression and identity. They reflect the island's diverse heritage, blending elements of Spanish, African, and indigenous influences into a rich tapestry of language and folklore. Many Cuban proverbs are steeped in metaphor and imagery, adding depth and nuance to their meanings and interpretations.

Whether used in everyday conversation, storytelling, or as a form of oral tradition, Cuban proverbs play a vital role in preserving and transmitting the cultural heritage of the island. They serve as a reminder of the values, beliefs, and customs that have shaped Cuban identity throughout the centuries, offering a glimpse into the soul of the nation and its people.

Preservation Efforts: Protecting Cuba's Heritage

Preservation efforts in Cuba are paramount to safeguarding the island's rich cultural and natural heritage for future generations. With its wealth of historic sites, diverse ecosystems, and unique cultural traditions, Cuba faces numerous challenges in preserving its heritage while navigating modern development and economic pressures.

One of the most significant preservation efforts in Cuba is the restoration and maintenance of its architectural heritage. The island is home to numerous historic cities and towns with well-preserved colonial-era buildings, many of which are UNESCO World Heritage Sites. Efforts are underway to restore and rehabilitate these architectural gems, ensuring that they remain intact for future generations to enjoy.

In addition to architectural preservation, Cuba is also focused on protecting its natural environment and biodiversity. The island boasts a diverse range of ecosystems, including lush rainforests, pristine beaches, and vibrant coral reefs. Conservation initiatives are in place to protect these fragile ecosystems from threats such as deforestation, pollution, and climate change, ensuring that Cuba's natural beauty remains intact for years to come.

Cultural preservation efforts in Cuba extend beyond tangible heritage to include intangible cultural practices and traditions. The island is known for its vibrant music, dance, and culinary traditions, which play a central role in Cuban identity and national pride. Cultural institutions and grassroots organizations work together to safeguard these traditions, promoting awareness and appreciation of Cuba's cultural heritage among both locals and visitors alike.

Another key aspect of preservation efforts in Cuba is education and awareness-building. Through public outreach programs, community engagement initiatives, and educational campaigns, efforts are made to raise awareness about the importance of preserving Cuba's heritage and the role that individuals can play in safeguarding it. By fostering a sense of pride and ownership in their cultural and natural heritage, Cuba aims to instill a collective responsibility for its preservation among its citizens.

International collaboration also plays a crucial role in preservation efforts in Cuba. The island has partnered with organizations such as UNESCO and the World Monuments Fund to implement conservation projects, share expertise, and access funding for heritage preservation initiatives. These partnerships enable Cuba to leverage external resources and expertise to address preservation challenges more effectively.

Overall, preservation efforts in Cuba are multifaceted and multifaceted, encompassing architectural, natural, and cultural heritage. By prioritizing conservation, education, and collaboration, Cuba is committed to protecting its rich heritage and ensuring that it remains a source of pride and inspiration for generations to come.

The Future of Cuba: Challenges and Opportunities

The future of Cuba is a topic of great significance and speculation, as the island nation grapples with a myriad of challenges and opportunities on the horizon. As Cuba moves forward into the 21st century, it faces both internal and external factors that will shape its trajectory in the years to come.

One of the foremost challenges facing Cuba is its economic situation. The country's socialist economy has long been plagued by inefficiencies, bureaucratic red tape, and limited access to foreign investment. Despite recent reforms aimed at opening up the economy to private enterprise and foreign investment, Cuba continues to struggle with low productivity, inadequate infrastructure, and reliance on outdated industries such as sugar and tobacco.

Another pressing issue facing Cuba is its political landscape. The island has been ruled by the Communist Party for over six decades, and while recent changes in leadership have raised hopes for political reform, the Cuban government remains tightly controlled and resistant to significant change. The lack of political freedom and civil liberties has led to tensions between the government and dissidents, as well as strained relations with the international community.

In addition to economic and political challenges, Cuba also faces environmental concerns that threaten its long-term sustainability. The island is vulnerable to the impacts of climate change, including rising sea levels, extreme weather events, and loss of biodiversity. Deforestation, pollution, and overdevelopment further exacerbate these challenges, posing a threat to Cuba's natural ecosystems and coastal communities.

Despite these challenges, Cuba also possesses significant opportunities for growth and development. The island's strategic location in the Caribbean, combined with its rich cultural heritage and natural beauty, makes it a prime destination for tourism and investment. With the easing of travel restrictions and the normalization of relations with the United States, Cuba has seen a surge in tourism and foreign investment in recent years, providing much-needed revenue and economic opportunities for its citizens.

Furthermore, Cuba's highly educated workforce and advanced healthcare system position it as a leader in fields such as biotechnology, medicine, and renewable energy. The island has made strides in developing its own vaccines, medications, and medical technologies, earning international recognition for its contributions to global health and innovation.

As Cuba looks to the future, it must navigate these challenges and opportunities with careful consideration and strategic planning. By addressing issues such as economic reform, political openness, environmental sustainability, and social equality, Cuba can position itself for long-term stability, prosperity, and success in the years ahead.

Epilogue

In closing, the story of Cuba is one of resilience, complexity, and enduring spirit. From its pre-colonial origins to its modern-day challenges and opportunities, Cuba's journey is a testament to the strength and determination of its people.

As we reflect on Cuba's history, we are reminded of the island's rich cultural heritage, shaped by centuries of Spanish colonial rule, African influence, and indigenous traditions. From its vibrant music and dance to its flavorful cuisine and colorful festivals, Cuba's cultural tapestry is a source of pride and inspiration for its citizens and visitors alike.

Throughout its history, Cuba has faced numerous challenges, including foreign invasions, economic hardships, and political turmoil. Yet, time and time again, the Cuban people have demonstrated their resilience and perseverance in the face of adversity, rallying together to overcome obstacles and shape their own destiny.

Today, as Cuba stands at a crossroads, it is poised to embrace a new era of change and transformation. With the recent easing of tensions with the United States and the gradual opening of its economy to foreign investment,

Cuba is entering a period of unprecedented opportunity and uncertainty.

However, as Cuba looks to the future, it must also confront pressing issues such as economic inequality, environmental sustainability, and political reform. These challenges will require bold leadership, innovative solutions, and inclusive dialogue to address effectively.

Despite the uncertainties that lie ahead, one thing remains certain: the spirit of Cuba will endure. Whether in its bustling streets of Havana, its tranquil countryside of Viñales, or its pristine beaches of Varadero, Cuba's beauty and resilience will continue to captivate and inspire generations to come.

As we bid farewell to Cuba, let us remember the lessons of its past, celebrate the triumphs of its present, and look forward with hope and optimism to the possibilities of its future. For in the heart of Cuba beats the spirit of a nation, steadfast and unyielding, ready to embrace whatever challenges and opportunities lie ahead.

Made in the USA
Las Vegas, NV
03 January 2025

15790777R00066